P9-CEV-630

Are you ready to turn the page and
start a new chapter in the American story?
—Pete Buttigieg

In honor of three memorable educators:
Janet Henley, Roy Nichols, and Connie Bilyeu
—R. S.
To the queer kids growing up in small towns everywhere
—L. H.

Henry Holt and Company, *Publishers since 1866*
Henry Holt® is a registered trademark of Macmillan Publishing Group, LLC
120 Broadway, New York, NY 10271 · mackids.com

Library of Congress Cataloging-in-Publication Data
Names: Sanders, Rob, author. | Hastings, Levi, illustrator.
Title: Mayor Pete : the story of Pete Buttigieg / by Rob Sanders ; illustrated by Levi Hastings.
Other titles: Story of Pete Buttigieg
Description: New York : Henry Holt Books for Young Readers, 2020 |
Series: Who did it first; 4 | Audience: Ages 4–8 | Audience: Grades2–3 |
Summary: "A picture book biography of Pete Buttigieg, mayor of
South Bend, Indiana, and 2020 presidential election hopeful." —Provided by publisher.
Identifiers: LCCN 2019037086 | ISBN 978-1-250-26757-3 (hardcover)
Subjects: LCSH: Buttigieg, Pete, 1982—Juvenile literature. | Mayors—Indiana—South Bend—Biography—Juvenile literature. |
South Bend (Ind.)—Politics and government—Juvenile literature. | Afghan War, 2001—Veterans—Biography—Juvenile literature. |
Gay men—Indiana—Biography—Juvenile literature. | South Bend (Ind.)—Biography—Juvenile literature. |
Presidents—United States—Election—2020—Juvenile literature.
Classification: LCC F534.S7 B878 2019 | DDC 977.2/89044092 [B]—dc23
LC record available at https://lccn.loc.gov/2019037086

Our books may be purchased in bulk for promotional, educational, or business use.
Please contact your local bookseller or the Macmillan Corporate and Premium Sales Department at
(800) 221-7945 ext. 5442 or by email at MacmillanSpecialMarkets@macmillan.com.

First edition, 2020 / Designed by Angela Jun
The illustrations for this book were created digitally on an iPad.
Printed in China by RR Donnelley Asia Printing Solutions Ltd., Dongguan City, Guangdong Province

1 3 5 7 9 10 8 6 4 2

MAYOR PETE

THE STORY OF PETE BUTTIGIEG

ROB SANDERS ✦ Illustrated by **LEVI HASTINGS**

A WHO DID IT FIRST? BOOK

HENRY HOLT AND COMPANY
NEW YORK

He was born while a record-setting snowstorm blanketed South Bend, Indiana.

Joseph and Jennifer Anne proudly welcomed Peter Paul Montgomery Buttigieg—or Pete—home.

Only time would tell who the boy in the two-story house on College Street would become.

Pete grew up in a neighborhood
filled with tree-lined streets, dogs,
and kids. It was a place where families
looked out for one another.

On his way to school, he passed
by abandoned, crumbling factories
and watched trains rumble through
town on their way to somewhere else.

Saturdays in the fall were filled with the roar of football fans at the University of Notre Dame's stadium.

Watching football games with his dad, Pete learned about losing and winning.

South Bend itself was a city of losses and wins.

Over time, Pete's hometown had lost the factories that made it prosperous decades before.

But South Bend had also won, as it became a well-known college town.

Of course, as a boy, Pete didn't spend a lot of time thinking about those things. He was busy with school and friends, piano lessons and homework, visiting Notre Dame's campus with his professor parents, playing at Triangle Park, and dreaming of being an astronaut.

Corn-harvesting autumns turned
into snowy, cardinal-dotted winters.

Tulip poplar–filled springs
swirled into firefly summers.

By the time Pete entered high school, he was studying new languages and a new instrument—the guitar.

He joined a garage band, played a few gigs, and even built his own guitar.

But something else was plucking away at Pete's mind—public service. He was beginning to wonder how a boy from South Bend could help others.

Pete decided to try his hand at high school politics.

The office: student body treasurer.

The outcome: defeat.

But Pete's dream of being a leader didn't end.

He ran for another position: senior class president.

A different campaign.

A different outcome.

Pete won!

Only time would tell who the boy attending
Saint Joseph High School would become.

Pete worked hard in high school and was involved in school activities and clubs. His grades were good. He applied to colleges, hoping to get into Harvard University.

When snow melted into spring and peony buds burst into fragrant blooms, Pete put on a cap and gown. High school graduation had arrived.

By the time the corn was tall and ready to pick, Pete's college hopes had grown into reality. He headed off to Harvard University in Cambridge, Massachusetts.

He studied history and literature, worked as an intern at the John F. Kennedy Presidential Library, and continued to practice and learn languages—French, Spanish, Maltese, and Arabic.

Above one of the gates at Harvard, Pete read these words:

ENTER TO GROW IN WISDOM.

On the opposite side of the gate were the words:

DEPART TO SERVE BETTER THY COUNTRY AND THY KIND.

For the next decade, those words seemed to guide
Pete's choices.

He perfected Arabic in the steaming heat of Tunis.
He studied philosophy, politics, and economics at
Pembroke College, surrounded by the towering
spires of Oxford, England.

He worked in the windy city of Chicago, learning about business.

But throughout those ten years, as new ideas filled his brain, one thought never left Pete's mind—public service.

Each of his experiences, all of his travels, and his years of learning brought Pete closer and closer to serving others.

Like the wind pushes snow into drifts, something was pushing at Pete. Or maybe something was pulling him back to where it all began: South Bend, Indiana.

Soon Pete decided to try his hand at politics again.

The office: Indiana state treasurer.

The outcome: defeat.

But just like in high school, Pete's dream of being a leader didn't end.

He ran for another position: mayor of South Bend.

A different campaign.

A different outcome.

Pete won!

Only time would tell who the mayor
of South Bend would become.

Pete had learned a lot about winning and losing. Now Mayor Pete's job was to make sure South Bend and its citizens won more and lost less.

From checking on plows during a snowstorm to helping his city recover from spring floods, from celebrating South Bend's 150th anniversary to enjoying Apple Days each fall, Mayor Pete served his city every day.

Being mayor was a big job with big responsibilities.
But sometimes being mayor meant just showing up
and helping out.

Mayor Pete officiated
wedding ceremonies.

He presided at
ribbon cuttings.

He read to second graders.

South Bend became a city with a
new outlook, a hometown for innovative
industries, and a community that
welcomed all people—no matter their
age, race, gender, religion, culture, or
sexual orientation.

As freezing temperatures crept through South Bend once again, Pete was called into even more important service.

He was deployed to Afghanistan as a member of the Navy Reserves.

Trading in his suit and tie for fatigues, Pete drove and guarded soldiers in convoys along crowded, dangerous city streets.

The work took flexibility, teamwork, and communication.

This service wasn't about winning and losing.

This service was about life and death.

When Mayor Pete safely returned to South Bend, there was another campaign to begin.

A reelection campaign.

During this run for office, Pete decided the time had come to make an announcement.

He had stood up for the rights of others but had never told the whole truth about himself.

He wrote an essay for the local paper.

As the sun rose on a June morning, folks sipped their coffee and read the news.

"I am gay . . . ," Pete told all of South Bend and all of the world. "It's just a fact of life, like having brown hair, and part of who I am."

Being honest about who he was, was a win for Pete.

Many, however, were sure it would mean a loss as mayor.

Only time would tell who the gay man
running for reelection would become.

When the votes were counted on election night, Pete won.

And he won big.

Pete's work as mayor continued.

There were challenges and victories.

Wins and losses.

And there was something new . . .

. . . or some*one* new.

Pete met a teacher named Chasten Glezman.

A friendship sprouted between the two men.

And like Indiana sweet corn, a relationship began to grow.

Frozen ground thawed into planting season; summer sun
and rain produced autumn's harvest.

Over time, the mayor and the schoolteacher fell in love.

They shared a home.

They adopted dogs.

They were married.

Mayor Pete continued his work and his service,
now with a husband and partner by his side.

Soon a new idea began to grow in Pete's mind.

An almost impossible idea.

On another snowy day in South Bend, Indiana, Pete began to explore the possibility of running for a different office.

He spoke and listened. He appeared on television and in newspapers.

He talked about what America could be.

People started to pay attention.

Then, on a rainy April day, Pete stood before a crowd
in what used to be one of South Bend's abandoned factories.
Something new was growing inside the old building—
   a campaign,
   a desire to serve,
   a feeling of anticipation and excitement.

"My name is Pete Buttigieg. They call me Mayor Pete," he said. "I am a proud son of South Bend, Indiana, and I am running for president of the United States."

"We live in a moment that compels us each to act," Pete told the cheering crowd. "You and I have the chance to usher in a new American spring."

Only time will tell who Pete Buttigieg, presidential candidate, will become.

"At the beginning of this decade, it was certain in my state that you could either serve in elected office or you could be out, but not both. When I joined the military, it was a matter of law that you could either be in uniform or you could be out, but not both. As recently as a few years ago, in most states, you could be in a same-sex relationship or you could be married, but not both. And today, in that same decade, it is possible for a war veteran and top-tier presidential candidate to campaign with his husband at his side."
—Mayor Pete Buttigieg, June 2019

★ ★ ★

MAYOR PETE'S PLACE IN HISTORY

Pete Buttigieg has already made history. He is the first millennial (a person born between 1982 and 2004) to run for president of the United States. He is the first out and proud gay candidate for the Democratic nomination and the first candidate married to a partner of the same gender. Mayor Pete is also the only veteran of the Afghanistan war to run for the highest office in the land. Time will tell what other history Pete Buttigieg will make.

HOW DO YOU SAY THAT NAME?

Pete Buttigieg has spent a lot of time telling people how to pronounce his last name. (The origin of the name is Maltese, from the country of Malta.) Pete says *BOOT-edge-edge*. However, his husband, Chasten Glezman Buttigieg, prefers the pronunciation *BUDdha-judge* or *BOOT-a-judge*. The difficult name may be the reason many folks simply call him Mayor Pete.

WHO CAN BE PRESIDENT?

The requirements to be president of the United States are found in one of the nation's original and most important documents: the United States Constitution. Article II, Section 1, of the Constitution says:

> *No person except a natural born citizen, or a citizen of the United States, at the time of the adoption of this Constitution, shall be eligible to the office of president; neither shall any person be eligible to that office who shall not have attained to the age of thirty-five years, and been fourteen years a resident within the United States.*

In other words, a person elected as president must have been born in the United States, must be at least thirty-five years old, and must have lived in the United States for at least fourteen years. Pete Buttigieg meets all those requirements.

He was born in South Bend, Indiana, USA, and when he announced his candidacy for president, he was thirty-seven years old. Except for a few years living abroad for college and serving in the military in Afghanistan, Pete has always lived in the United States.

PETE BUTTIGIEG—A TIME LINE

January 19, 1982
Born in South Bend, Indiana, to Joseph A. Buttigieg and
Jennifer Anne Montgomery

2000
Graduates from St. Joseph High School in South Bend

2000–2004
Attends Harvard University and receives a Bachelor of
Arts degree in history and literature

2004
Works as a research director for Senator John Kerry's
presidential campaign

2004–2005
Works as a conference director for the Cohen Group

2005–2007
Attends Pembroke College at Oxford University and
receives a Bachelor of Arts in philosophy, politics, and
economics

2007–2010
Works as an associate with McKinsey & Company

September 2009
Takes the oath of military service and becomes an ensign,
or entry–level commissioned officer, for the United States
Navy Reserve

November 2, 2010
Loses the race for Indiana state treasurer

November 8, 2011
Elected mayor of South Bend, Indiana

January 1, 2012
Takes the oath of office, becoming the thirty–second mayor
of South Bend

February 28, 2014
Reports for a seven–month US Naval Reservist deployment
in Afghanistan

September 25, 2014
Returns to South Bend and his mayoral duties

June 16, 2015
Comes out as gay in an op–ed in the *South Bend Tribune*

November 3, 2015
Reelected as mayor

January 5, 2015
Announces he will run for chairman of the Democratic
National Committee

February 25, 2015
Drops out of the race for the chairmanship

June 16, 2018
Marries Chasten Glezman

December 17, 2018
Announces he will not run again for the position of South
Bend mayor

January 23, 2019
Announces he is forming an exploratory committee for a
possible run for president of the United States

April 14, 2019
Announces he is running for president

Photo by Gary Riggs/ Courtesy of Wikimedia Commons

SELECTED SOURCES

Bauer, Caleb, and Grace McDermott. "Pete Buttigieg Fans Ignore Rain,
Cold as They Crowd Downtown South Bend for Announcement."
South Bend Tribune, April 15, 2019. southbendtribune.com/news
/local/pete-buttigieg-fans-ignore-rain-cold-as-they-crowd
-downtown/article_8576b1e8-b5b9-5da4-872d-e8574644fd36.html.

Burns, Alexander. "Pete Buttigieg's Campaign Kickoff: Full Speech,
Annotated." *The New York Times*, April 15, 2019. nytimes
.com/2019/04/15/us/politics/pete-buttigieg-speech.html.

Buttigieg, Pete. "I launched a presidential exploratory committee."
Twitter, January 23, 2019. twitter.com/petebuttigieg/status
/1088016937718874112?lang=en.

Buttigieg, Pete. *Shortest Way Home: One Mayor's Challenge and
a Model for America's Future.* New York: Liveright Publishing
Corporation, 2019.

Buttigieg Pete. "South Bend Mayor: Why Coming Out Matters." *South
Bend Tribune*, June 16, 2015. southbendtribune.com/news/local
/south-bend-mayor-why-coming-out-matters/article_4dce0d12-1415
-11e5-83c0-739eebd623ee.html.

Colbert, Stephen. "Pete Buttigieg: The Case for a Younger President."
The Late Show with Stephen Colbert, February 25, 2019. youtube.com
/watch?v=u7SHQSGesyM.

"From Youngest Mayor to Smart Streets: A Timeline of Buttigieg's
Political Career." *South Bend Tribune*, December 17, 2018.
southbendtribune.com/news/local/from-youngest-mayor-to
-smart-streets-a-timeline-of-pete/article_74f5ca74-ddb4-5bc3-915f
-a4773c7db8f8.html.

"Mayor Pete Buttigieg '05—from South Bend to Oxford . . . and Back."
The North American Pembrokian, March 23, 2015. pcfna.org/?p=632.

"We the Kids Interview with Pete Buttigieg, Mayor of South Bend, IN."
We the Kids, August 2019. youtube.com/watch?v=d3EugqJRqlw.

Wertz, Nathan. "Vets in Public Service: South Bend Mayor Pete
Buttigieg." *Military.com*, October 16, 2018. military.com
/undertheradar/2018/10/15/vets-public-service-south-bend-mayor
-pete-buttigieg.html.